"I enjoyed the format and the fashion in which the story is delivered and found the content and message to be insightful and, from a practical sense, useful. An easy read with a powerful message."
—Karl R. Wolcott, Chief Operating Officer, Ridgeway Biosystems, Inc.

"A lot of lip service has been paid to achieving personal/professional balance in our lives. Chuck's new book provides practical, concrete steps we can take to actually approach that balance, and in so doing help our organizations compete successfully."
—John E. Sircy, President, Henry A. Petter Supply Company

"*Coffee at Luna's* is a really excellent read, both my fiancée and I agreed. He said 'this book is describing my life for the past 10 years!' We both found the book very practical, realistic, and relevant, and very good advice. We will certainly apply the principles in both our work and personal lives."
—Alisa Oswalt, Manager, Unisys Corporation

"*Coffee at Luna's* paints a vivid picture of our high-speed society and A types trying to make a difference. It touched close to home for me and was a thought-provoking reminder of the importance of balance in our lives. I particularly liked the renewable aspect to the strategy presented. So often, we are presented a plan for success in our lives and careers but it fails to include that key renewable component. The power of recognition and the simple thank you cannot be overstated; this fable makes that abundantly clear."
—Don West, Managing Director, State National Insurance

"The greatest thing about this book is that it doesn't have to replace any other change efforts that are already underway, such as Redesign or Six Sigma—it is a perfect and practical complement to any of them."
—Tom Murach, Banking Industry Executive

"A quick, easy read. Been there and know people there today. 'Stop, look, listen' is intuitive and basic leadership but so easy to ignore."
—Gerald Thompson, Senior Director, Strategic Sourcing,
Florida Power & Light

"The fundamentals are timeless truths whose depths can be explored over a lifetime. The use of the mystical Teacher is awesome and the choice of characters captures many people in real life."
—Bill Chamberland, Manager, A State Agency

"GREAT business fable (hear my applause!). It's just the kind of medicine that businesses and their burned-out employees need today."
—Shannon Ingram, Writer/Editor

"In *Coffee at Luna's*, Chuck Martin has taken lessons of our childhood of Stop, Look, and Listen and expanded them with a focus on the business world geared to releasing the energy and enthusiasm of the whole team toward success. Utilizing these three easy steps can change your life and the lives of all around you."
—Timothy J. Smith, Logistics Executive

"Congratulations to Chuck for an amazing story line with depth. Upon my first reading, I would recommend that all companies of any size purchase a copy for each employee. After re-reading *Coffee at Luna's*, I plan to give a copy to my son, Ed, and his friends, Mike, Craig, and Dave, who are definitely in need of a Teacher in their young corporate world journey."
—Carolyn Dickson, Sales & Marketing,
BFI Waste Services of Fresno

Coffee at Luna's

A Business Fable

**Three Secrets to Knowledge,
Self-Improvement, and Happiness
In Your Work and Life**

Books by Chuck Martin

TOUGH MANAGEMENT: The 7 Ways to Make
Tough Decisions Easier, Deliver the Numbers,
and Grow Business in Good Times and Bad
(McGraw-Hill)

MANAGING FOR THE SHORT TERM:
The New Rules for Running a Business in a
Day-to-Day World (Doubleday)

NET FUTURE: The seven cybertrends that will
drive your business, create new wealth, and define
your future (McGraw-Hill)

THE DIGITAL ESTATE: Strategies for Competing,
Surviving, and Thriving in an Internetworked World
(McGraw-Hill)

MAX-e-MARKETING IN THE NET FUTURE:
The Imperatives for Outsmarting the Competition
in the Net Economy (co-author): (McGraw-Hill).

Coffee at Luna's

A Business Fable

By

Chuck Martin

**Three Secrets to Knowledge,
Self-Improvement, and Happiness
In Your Work and Life**

NFI Research
North Hampton, New Hampshire

Dedicated to Teri, my wife, for so much love, encouragement, and for giving me perspective about what truly matters. And to my sons Ryan and Chase, for giving me reason to keep that perspective.

PUBLISHED BY NFI RESEARCH
North Hampton, New Hampshire

For further information
603-964-3930
www.nfiresearch.com

Cover and book design by Arrow Graphics, Inc.
Watertown, Massachusetts
Printed in the United States of America

First Edition

ISBN: 0-9763273-0-9

Library of Congress Control Number: 2004098585

10 9 8 7 6 5 4 3 2 1

"Brian, this is Walter. I need some serious help. My boss just quit and his boss wants me to take the job. I know it's over my head and this department is in critical condition. Call me as soon as you can."

When Brian got home and retrieved the message he called his friend Walter.

The two men went way back, having grown up in the same neighborhood as childhood friends. Although their careers took them in different directions, they stayed in close touch.

It was about a year ago that Brian was promoted at his company. Walter couldn't help but notice that shortly after the promotion his friend dramatically changed—for the better.

He had become very cheerful, relaxed, and highly successful at his job. They never talked about it, but Walter now needed some of whatever Brian had.

"Hey, congratulations Walter! Just got your message. That's great news about the promotion."

"Thanks for the good words, but I'm not sure I'm really up to it. I mean, this place is a disaster, people are quitting all over the place, and morale is in the toilet, mine included."

"Don't panic, Walter. You'll do just fine."

"Easy for you to say, Brian, with everything going your way. By the way, why are things going so well for you? You always seem to be smiling, you always call me back right away, and you're, well, really successful. What's your secret?"

"You wouldn't believe me if I told you."

"Hey, I'm desperate. If you have any ideas that might help, I'm all ears."

"Well, I was in a similar situation some time back and a friend told me a story that turned everything around for me."

"After I heard this tale, I found the steps to take to create much more balance between work and home, became dramatically more in tune with everyone around me, and totally re-focused on what I wanted to accomplish in my life."

"Wow, that must have been some story!"

"Yes, it was a story of a manager who was in over his head and then learned a very simple way to improve himself and create happiness in work and life immediately."

"I took some important lessons from that story and adapted them for me. People around me noticed a positive change right away."

"So the story helped me a lot and I attribute it to my success today."

"Really? Just lessons from a story?"

"Yes, that was it. Now I'm much more aware of what's going on around me at work, and I spend much less time with my head down. I have more time to think and am doing much more with less."

"The fable changed my life for the better. It made me happier and inspired me to help others and myself like never before. Although it was mainly a story about work, it even changed my personal life."

"I now spend more quality time with my family, I'm more confident and, believe it or not, I work fewer hours than I did before."

"As I said, Brian, I'm all ears."

"Well, different people can take different lessons away from the story, but it was an eye-opener for me. I didn't realize how much I was actually missing in my life, not just in my work. I'm not sure if it will hit you the same way, but the story taught me that it only takes a few small changes to become more productive, more balanced, and a whole lot happier."

"Brian, you *must* tell me the whole thing. Now I desperately want to hear whatever tale it is."

"OK, if you want, I'll tell you the story and hopefully you can take some lessons from it that might help you tackle everything more positively and make you see how to appreciate more around you."

"Brian, it sounds like I really need this story."

OK, but on one condition. You will have to share the same story someday with someone else when they need help. Agreed?"

"Agreed."

Brian started to share with his friend the tale of Coffee at Luna's.

Bill Taylor had worked for UniShare Technologies Inc. for six months, after spending four years at a smaller computer software company and three years at a computer consulting firm.

He settled into his new job fairly easily, though moving from San Francisco to Boston took some adjustment.

Over time, the work pace became as intense as usual for Bill, with 10-hour days and little time during the day for anything personal. He began to feel the stress.

The most difficult adjustment for Bill was getting used to the cold and snowy winter. When Bill and his wife Jessica decided on the move they reasoned that they'd get used to the winters, at least eventually.

Now in month three of winter, they were still awaiting that adjustment.

It was one of those cold, snowy days that Bill's boss, Ted Hopkins, called him in to chat.

"Bill, we've been watching you and have been fairly impressed with your work. You follow orders well and, for the most part, meet your deadlines. We have also noticed how hard you seem to be working. However, to succeed long term here takes something a bit different."

"I don't know what you mean, Mr. Hopkins. Are you saying I'm not working hard enough? I'm putting in more than 60 hours a week! I've worked every Saturday since I started working here. I work more hours than anyone in my group."

"I answer my voice mail and email around the clock. I always respond right away and I check voice mail all weekend. I'm even available during vacation."

Bill was starting to feel irate. "How can you say I don't deliver for this company, it's all I do."

"No, it's not that Bill. We know you're working long and hard and we appreciate it. You obviously have a lot to offer the company. You just need a little something more to make you truly succeed long-term here."

Ted could see the look of hurt on Bill's face. On the other hand, he could see that Bill was physically exhausted and highly stressed and this would not be the time for the discussion he had in mind.

"Bill, we want you to succeed. Look, nothing is going to happen between now and the beginning of the week, so why not take some time over the weekend and get some rest and let's talk again on Monday. How about first thing in the morning, say, 10 o'clock?"

"Yeah, 10 will be fine. See you then."

Bill left totally dejected, went to his office and grabbed his coat for his dismal half-hour drive home.

The drive gave him a lot of time to think.

What's he talking about? I've been busting my butt for this company for six months and now they say I'm lacking something. I hardly ever see my family since I started work here. I missed more than half my son's soccer games because of work. I eat lunch at my desk every day.

And they aren't happy with me? Time to start looking around. Maybe a warmer climate would be better anyway.

What am I going to tell Jessica? It was a tough sell to get her to leave the West Coast. And what about our son? We tore Peter away from all his friends in San Francisco when he was only 10 and now we're going to do that again?

I'm outta here as soon as I can find another job. What's he talking about missing something? I'll show him missing something. They'll be missing me. Let's see how well they can do without me. I carry my department. They don't really know how much work I really do there. They'll see.

Just wait till Monday. First thing? 10 o'clock is first thing for him? I'm in at 7 every day and he says let's meet first thing at 10? At 10! The guy's a lunatic. Why did I ever take this job? And the move. How can I tell Jessica we have to move again?

Well, at least I didn't get fired. Or maybe I did? Maybe they're telling me to look around. Maybe I can get a severance package; at least we'd have some breathing room. What about the mortgage and the car payments?

We don't have enough saved. I knew I should have saved more each paycheck. And the car payments. Maybe we can get by with one car. But how would Jessica get around? And how would we pick up Peter at school?

How long could it take to get another job? I could go back to my old company. Not really. They filled my position. And it was as much of a sweatshop as UniShare.

So how did UniShare get such a good reputation as a great place to work? Some great place. Sixty-plus hours a week for six months and what do I get? Nothing. Fired. Tossed out onto the street.

What am I going to do?

Bill arrived home after what seemed like the blink of an eye. At least it was Friday. Bill decided on the spot he would not go to the office on Saturday. Maybe just get some sleep. He was exhausted.

"Hi, Bill, how was your day?"

"I've had better, Jess. What's for dinner?"

"Canned ham."

"Perfect."

Bill went to bed early, but didn't sleep much. All he could think about was the upcoming Monday meeting and what he was going to say.

Instead of his usual 7 a.m. Saturday trip to the office, Bill decided to catch up on his backlog of email and organize his computer filing system.

By 10 o'clock, Bill had spent three hours at his computer and felt he hadn't even made a dent. Jessica stuck her head into Bill's home office to see if he wanted to go with her and Peter to the mall to get Peter some new cleats for Sunday's game.

"No, I have to catch up on some work, but go ahead and we'll hook up later." Bill ended up working Sunday as well. He missed Peter's soccer game, but at least he got his email organized, his office voice mailbox emptied, and even managed to better organize his home office.

Bill was nervous about the Monday meeting, especially since he felt he had been making such a great contribution to the company. He certainly didn't feel he had done anything wrong, but he knew life was not always fair.

Bill was on the road to the office by 6:30 a.m., *his* typical "first thing" in the morning. After a few hours of busywork, Bill headed over to Corporate for what he viewed as a mid-day meeting.

Ted immediately got up to greet Bill as soon as he saw him.

"Good to see you, Bill. Come in. How was your weekend?"

He trashes my entire weekend then has the nerve to ask how it was? This is sure going to be some meeting.

"It was fine."

"Let me get right to the point. As I mentioned on Friday, we've been watching you these past few months and we've been impressed with your work."

"But I thought…"

"I know Bill, I could see you thought something was wrong at our brief meeting on Friday, so I wanted you to rest over the weekend so we could tackle what we have to discuss with fresh minds."

"As you know, this company has been expanding dramatically the last few years. We've been hiring rather quickly and absorbing the talent as best we know how."

"We've also been making several acquisitions, and later today it will be announced that we've just purchased Grand View Connections, a small software company in Cambridge, just across the Charles River."

"Grand View had gotten itself into some financial trouble the past few years and morale there is pretty low. We have a new challenge for you if you feel up to it. The head of Grand View is leaving and we'd like you to take his spot. Of course, we'll support you if you need any help."

"Grand View will become a division of UniShare, and the employees there will immediately become UniShare employees."

Bill was stunned. Rather than being fired, he was being promoted!

"I don't know what to say. I'll do my best."

Events proceeded pretty rapidly from there. Bill went from cleaning out his old office on Monday to meeting with management Tuesday to starting in Cambridge on Wednesday. He was introduced to his new team by Mark Jordan, the senior vice president in charge of the acquisition.

Before he knew it, Bill was running an entire division of UniShare. Granted, it was a small group in relation to the overall size of UniShare, with only several dozen employees. But he figured its contribution to the overall company might be noticed if he increased it dramatically. Bill was excited and viewed this as a great career opportunity.

What Bill didn't realize was what a hornets' nest he was walking into.

By Friday, three employees had given their notice, all having been quickly recruited by Grand View's main competitor.

Bill hadn't even yet personally met with each member of the staff.

By week two, the pace of work had really picked up. There was little time for chitchat as Bill kept his head down focusing on meeting his first revenue targets.

It's all about the numbers, Bill kept telling himself. *We have to make the numbers.*

Trouble was, no matter how many ways Bill looked at the costs, production schedule, and sales figures, there was no way his group was going to make the numbers this time around. Bill started to feel panicked.

By the second month, Bill's days were getting longer and longer and he saw no light at the end of the tunnel.

They trust me with this new group and I can't even make the first quarterly numbers. They're going to think I can't handle it. I have to make the numbers. Even if everyone has to work seven days a week, we'll make those numbers.

Bill was falling behind and found that the only time he could get anything done was before and after the *official* workday hours of 9 and 5, so he started extending his workday on both ends.

He was leaving for the office by 6 a.m. every day and not getting home until after 8 o'clock each night.

He started going in on Saturdays again, figuring he could catch up then. His managers discovered this, so they also started working Saturdays, for more *face time* with the boss.

Bill was working more hours a week than he ever had and was getting less done. Even worse, he wasn't enjoying it at all. His family was getting used to him always being distracted while at home whenever he was there.

UniShare was the kind of company that expected a lot from its managers and employees and was clearly destined to grow to the size of a Fortune 500 company.

In return, the top employees were compensated well and seemed to stay with the company for a long time. Bill figured the top execs had to be making individual fortunes, since he reasoned that if he was working this hard as a manager in a small division, then they must be working around the clock.

The good news was that the majority of the managers Bill inherited from the last company knew their areas and were good at what they each did.

There was Michael Jensen, who had worked his way up to head the top team of software developers. Michael was a bit older than Bill, and thought he should have been given the job of division head. After all, he had been with the company since the beginning and always did what he was told to do.

Stephanie Rogers was relatively new to the company, but she impressed Bill with how organized she was. She was always first at a meeting, always took notes, and quietly did her work.

Though she impressed him, Bill couldn't help but notice that she came in late from time to time. He figured she probably partied hard some nights and just needed time to catch up. But she did her work so Bill figured he could live with it.

Then there was Ronald. Ronald Wetherbie. Bill viewed him as the company space cadet: always daydreaming, always late for meetings, never on time for anything.

Ronald had been with Grand View since college. Bill guessed he had never been managed well.

Although he didn't often agree with some of the decisions by the executives over the years, Ronald usually went along for the most part. When a decision didn't make sense to him, he basically ignored it, though not openly.

There were times that an edict would come from the president of the company, which Ronald knew would make no sense to his customers, so he never passed it along. He figured his one little area wouldn't make any difference and it wouldn't be noticed at the top. He was right.

Unfortunately, this had happened all over the company. This resulted in a total lack of efficiency, which meant that what the bosses were saying needed to get done wasn't getting done.

This ultimately translated into less efficiency, less revenue, and less profit. The spiral went on for years, as the company lost more and more business.

Eventually, the company got into trouble and UniShare saw an opportunity, so it bought it at a low price and sent Bill in to rebuild it.

These were the key people Bill had inherited. Everyone else seemed to come in on time, do his or her job, and go home on time. Bill would need more from all of them. There was just no way he could turn this group around without everyone's help, though he wasn't sure how he would get them each to work harder and more than they already were.

By the end of the second month, Bill figured he should get to better know everyone in the department and for them all to understand Bill's expectations of them.

He called all the employees and managers together for a meeting.

"I just want to say that I'm very glad to be here and will be working very hard to make this division successful."

"I also expect that all of you will work hard as well. We have a lot to do here."

"So, does anyone have any questions?"

Silence.

They're just staring. I guess I blew it. What can I say now? This is my first speech to the staff and I tanked. I want to get out of here.

"Good, then. Let's all get back to work."

As people filed out, Bill asked Stephanie to stay behind.

"Stephanie, let me ask you, why was everyone so quiet? I mean, no questions at all?"

"Well, it's first thing Monday and maybe people are tired from busy weekends."

"Yeah, you're probably right. OK, see you around."

As Stephanie left, Bill headed back to his office.

By the third month, Bill was feeling discouraged and exhausted from working so many hours. It was late Friday afternoon after a very long week that Bill got a call from Mark Jordan, the senior VP.

"So how are things going across the River, Bill?"

"Well, OK, I guess. But I need to give you a heads up that it doesn't look like we'll be on track to hit the revenue targets we agreed to for the first half of the year. But I'm sure trying."

"Yes, we know you are Bill. We have all the confidence in the world in you. On Monday, you'll get a visit from someone who over the years has taught us all at Corporate quite a lot. We think he might be able to help you as well, so just keep an open mind and it'll all work out. Have a great weekend, Bill, and get some rest!"

Bill slept well into both Saturday and Sunday mornings. He felt totally fried.

He came in at 7 on Monday and an elderly gentleman was waiting for him at his office.

"Hello, Bill. I've been sent here to help you."

"Welcome... sorry, I missed your name."

"My unofficial title is The Teacher. But you can just call me Teacher, because that has become my nickname."

"Well, Teacher, at this point, I can use all the help I can get. Has Corporate shown you the numbers? You probably know our run rate is down, sales are down, staffing is down, and profit is basically non-existent. So where would you like to start? You want to see the numbers? Or next month's projections?"

"Let's go have coffee at Luna's."

What? My department is falling apart, I'm totally under the gun, and this guy wants to go out for coffee? Is he kidding? Though at this stage I have nothing to lose. Corporate endorses him so it'll be their fault if this doesn't work out.

"Sure, Luna's would be fine."

Find It

As they sat and sipped cappuccino, Teacher said nothing.

"So, what is your specialty?" Bill asked. "Finance? Software development? Manufacturing? What? And how long will you be with us? A day? A week?"

"My specialty is helping people, Bill. And I'll be with you until you feel comfortable with three key secrets to be successful."

"There are three secrets to success? Someone should have told me sooner," Bill laughed.

"Well, Bill, they have taken some time to learn, but I've been sent here to pass them along to you."

"OK, Teacher, so what's the first thing? It must be about a better way to make the numbers, right? Or is it a way to get people to work harder? So what do I do?"

"You're doing it."

"Doing what? I'm just sitting here drinking coffee. I'm doing absolutely nothing!"

"That's right, Bill. You're doing nothing. You have *stopped*. This will allow you to *Find It*."

"Find what?"

"Find the knowledge that is all around you so that you can better understand what is going on."

"I don't know what you mean."

"Well, Bill, the first step in making everything around you better is to understand what, in fact, is going on around you. To *find it*, you have to take time to look for it."

"The way to do this is to *stop, look, and listen* so you can truly understand what is going on. This will allow you to *find it*."

"You mean I have to stop work?"

"Well, no, not really. Look at it this way."

"If you're driving your car in a busy city and you come to a stop sign, you *stop*. You then take in the entire situation around you, and you see if someone is crossing in front of you. Before you go, you look both ways, and you become aware of all your surroundings. "

"The same holds true in business and in life. People today are going so fast and working so hard they sometimes forget to balance their lives. People are spending so much time with their heads down that they never look up to understand what is going on. They miss changes, they miss opportunities, and they miss many chances to provide more benefit to those around them."

"As more people keep their heads down, business and individuals become more insular and more alone. This affects both business and personal lives, although it tends to start at work."

"The majority of people in business today actually feel that most people in business are unbalanced, meaning their work is all consuming."

"This isn't healthy for the individual and it isn't healthy for the company where they work. When there is unbalance in work-home life, the person, the family, and the company all suffer. There is no true winner."

Bill thought a moment. "I must say, Teacher, that I don't think I've been very balanced these last few months. All I do is work. And the more I work it seems like the more I have to work. It's a never-ending cycle. So how do I change it? Where do I start?"

"First, you have to devise ways to *stop* yourself. When was the last time you took a two-hour lunch break?"

Bill laughed. "You really are funny, Teacher. I can't recall ever taking a two-hour lunch in my life! No one in my group has ever taken a two-hour lunch, as far as I can tell. We have too much to do."

"That's exactly the point. As you do more and more without *stopping*, you become less efficient. So that 10-minute issue takes 15 minutes. That 45-minute meeting lasts an hour."

"Then the day gets longer as you try to fit everything in. You work more hours to try to get it all done."

"The reality is that the two hours you might take to re-charge instead are being wasted during the course of the day anyway."

"People today need more time to think. It's tough to think about much while driving a car on the Autobahn at 90 miles an hour, with everyone trying to pass each other. You end up thinking only about how to keep the car on the road."

"Life is like that as well. We get caught up in doing more and doing it faster and we sometimes sacrifice quality and part of the precious time we have."

"You then lose perspective because you're tired or too focused on details to see the bigger picture. You're tired at work and you're tired at home. You feel like all you can do with your off time is to work even more to try to catch up, and your personal life takes a back seat. Those around you start to pull back because you become less and less attentive to them and on it goes."

"It's a downward spiral, from which there is no escape. Unless you *stop*!"

"You pretty well just described me. It's pretty depressing when you look at it that way."

"There's nothing to be depressed about Bill, because now you know about it."

"Now, *stopping* involves more than just taking a two-hour lunch hour. And you wouldn't want to do that every day."

"To *stop* requires you to repeatedly and continually pull back from whatever it is that makes you keep your head down."

"If you are spending four hours a day on email, stop using any email for a day or two. You'll notice that anything critical that was missed from email will be brought to your attention quickly."

"When you go on vacation, disconnect totally from work. Don't contact the office and don't let them contact you."

"Take a break and play golf or go have lunch with your kids. The least productive time for managers and executives is between 11 a.m. and 2 p.m. Those would be great tee times! It also would be a great time for a school lunch visit."

The point is, people don't take enough real breaks. The breaks can be a few minutes, a few hours, or even days or weeks."

"However, what is most important is what you do while you are *stopped*. You should look and listen to what is going on around you. This can't be done when you're working at 100 miles an hour."

"You can see this in the area of communications, one of the most critical shortfalls in business and life today."

"People generally feel that they communicate well, no matter who they are communicating to. However, many of them never check just what message was received. You'll be very surprised that when you *stop*, you have a much greater ability to determine if you really did communicate well, based on how well your message was understood."

"Makes sense," Bill said.

"Now let's get to specifics. Tell me about the people you work with."

Bill relayed his view of his three key players, Michael in development, the very organized Stephanie, and Ronald, the space cadet, who Bill considered to be the loner in the bunch.

He told Teacher about how he thought Michael felt he should have gotten Bill's job, how Stephanie comes in late several days a month, and how Ronald had always just sort of done his own thing.

"OK, for the rest of the day, I want you to make a point of observing what those three employees do in the course of the day. Nothing intrusive, just jot down your observations and we'll discuss them tomorrow."

"But what about work? I have a lot to do?"

"One day of *stopping* will be good for you. I assure you, the company will keep running. And the observations you gain will far outweigh any of the tasks you might have accomplished today."

As Teacher recommended, Bill spent the day out of his own office and did more roaming around the halls. Teacher gave him a strict directive not to do any of his work for a full day. After all, he was Teacher, and he was sent in by Corporate!

The next day, Teacher again was waiting for Bill at his office when he arrived for work, even though Bill didn't come in until 8 that day. Bill wondered if Teacher had been waiting an hour for him.

"Good morning, Bill. Shall we go to Luna's?"

"Sure, why not."

"Bring your notes."

Over coffee, Bill started to recount from his notes what he observed the previous day.

He told Teacher how he ran into Stephanie, who was surprised to see him at her desk. He recounted how he usually spent much of his time in his office, and had people come to him when he wanted to meet with them.

Bill described how he talked with Stephanie about why she is often late for work, and she told him it was because of medical appointments.

Teacher asked Bill the nature of Stephanie's medical issue but Bill said he didn't know. He didn't even ask, figuring it was personal.

"OK, Bill, let's stop here for a moment. Remember, to *find it*, you must first *stop, look*, and *listen*. You did great at the *stop* part. You didn't work in your office and you got out and about. That's very good. You looked and sought out Stephanie, that's also good.

But when it came to listening, it doesn't seem you heard everything she was saying."

"I don't get it Teacher. I heard everything she said, I even wrote most of it down."

She was trying to communicate more to you, but you failed to listen."

"OK, next."

Bill told how he dropped in on Michael Jensen, who had pretty much the same surprised-to-see-him reaction that Stephanie had. Michael went through all the projects he was working on. There was the software engineering project, the code development group report, the upcoming management report, and the staff evaluations, all in progress.

"Which one is Michael having the most problems with, Bill?"

"He didn't say."

"I see. And which one is the most critical for the overall business for, say, the next couple of years?"

"For the next couple of years? Well the code development always falls within its general time limits. And the management report always gets crunched through, even if by the last minute. I guess everything is really needed for the next month or so."

"What about the staff evaluations, Bill?"

"Oh, we can do those any time."

"Hold on a second, Bill. What is your division's biggest asset? I mean, what makes it valuable to UniShare?"

"Our great software products."

"OK, and who creates those products?"

"Everyone."

"OK, so let me understand this. The process of creating these products is more valuable than the people who actually create them?"

"Well, of course not."

"When you put staff evaluations – the measure of how well someone is creating what you say is the most important thing coming out of the division – at the bottom of the list of importance, what message does that send to those people?"

"I think I see your point."

"OK, and what about the third person, Ronald was it?"

"Oh, yes, that was probably the most interesting of the day. It turns out Ronald has two degrees and is quite bright. He actually created the most successful product in the early years of Grand View. He didn't get anything extra for the product's success, so he is a bit disgruntled, but he comes in every day and seems to do his work well."

How long ago was Grand View started?"

"More than 10 years ago, I think."

"OK." Teacher made a note in his book.

"Interestingly, Ronald happened to mention that some of the top people don't always appear to know what's going on at the customer level, based on the communications that come down the line. I guess maybe he was referring to the last leadership of the company. Maybe he was referring to me!"

"OK, Bill that was a great first day and a great start to finding it."

"Let's take a look at what you need to do to really get it. Today you should listen to learn and understand more about your three key people."

"For Stephanie, you should find out, in general, the magnitude of the medical issue that causes her to be late at times."

"For Michael, you should probe what troubles him the most. What, if anything, is it about his work that keeps him awake at night? It sounds like he has quite a lot on his plate and is under the gun for quarterly deadlines."

"And for Ronald, well, you may want to explore what he thinks the company should do differently, since he obviously doesn't think it's doing things correctly now."

"I can do that, but I'm really getting backed up on my work. "

"Don't worry about your work, the company will keep going."

That night, Bill got home early, a first for several months. He couldn't help notice his wife's surprised reaction, which was the same reaction he got the previous day when he visited Stephanie and Michael.

He started to think about how he really never *stopped, looked,* and *listened* around his family anymore. He was coming to the realization that he was not only buried at work, he was neglecting the needs of those he loved and who loved him most.

"Hey, Jess. What are you up to?"

"Just starting to make some dinner. And why are you home so early from work? That's not like you. I guess you'll be eating later, after you get your work done?"

"I don't have any work tonight. How about we go for a walk, if you have time before dinner? When will Peter be home?"

"Bill, it's Tuesday, Peter always has soccer practice after school on Tuesdays and I get him at the bus stop at 6:30."

"So let's walk then."

Bill started to tell Jessica about his last two days and the lessons he was starting to learn from Teacher. He told her how he felt he had gotten so caught up in his work that life was just passing him by and that he was missing a lot of the things that mattered."

He told her about the *stop, look,* and *listen* exercise he had gone through with his three key employees and his plans for the next day.

"Jess, I'm going to do this in our home life from now on too. I want to get more balanced. Peter will be an adult and I'll have missed his childhood."

Jessica was elated to hear Bill talk like this. She had been worried about how hard he had been working, but had vowed to herself that she would be totally supportive hoping things would eventually settle into some kind of normalcy.

For the past month, she had been telling Bill he was working too hard and warning him that it wasn't healthy long-term.

Lately she had been thinking that she would get used to the Boston winters sooner than their family life would become what she considered to be normal. At least Peter was doing well in school and had made a lot of new friends, and when Bill was not thinking about work he was always great to be with. Jessica and Bill loved each other very much, and had been through a lot together.

So what Bill was telling her now was incredibly good news to her.

"Well, I just wanted to share what's been going on. So what do you think?"

"It sounds absolutely great, Bill."

"But what?"

"But nothing!"

"Jess, tell me what you really think. I mean, really."

"Well, as you might have figured out, these past few months have been pretty hard on the family. Peter and I hardly ever see you. Well, we see you, but it's been like you haven't seen us."

"I just hope this new approach lasts. It isn't pleasant to feel like we're losing you to a job. I mean, how important is any job?"

"Thank you, Jess. I needed to hear that. No, this is for good. I'll never go back to the way it was, it just isn't worth it."

Bill had truly listened.

He figured he had one more person to shock and he was right, as Peter's face lit up like a Christmas tree when he saw his dad waiting for him at the bus stop later that evening.

That night Bill checked on Peter as he did his homework and even got to watch a movie with Jessica. He slept better than he had in months, to the point that he didn't make it to the office until just before 9 a.m. He had decided to take this *stop* thing seriously because it made total sense to him.

He just didn't understand why he hadn't figured this out by himself years ago. It seemed so simple, yet so profound.

I didn't think about it because I never took time to stop and think about it! How obvious!

Teacher was waiting at Bill's office when he arrived.

"So sorry I'm late," Bill blurted out instantly.

"You're not late Bill, I just got here."

"Oh good. Shall we go to Luna's? And I'll bring my notes."

"Well, Teacher you were right about not catching the whole story on the first day. I don't even know where to begin. Nothing was as it seemed."

"Just take them one at a time, Bill."

"Right. Stephanie's husband passed away two years ago, right after she started working for Grand View. It was a very difficult first year, especially raising their only child, a five-year old daughter named Lucy."

"About a year ago, Lucy was diagnosed with acute lymphocytic leukemia (ALL). The good news is that Stephanie expects Lucy to fully recover, but the poor child has to go through up to a year of chemotherapy treatments."

"I can't believe I thought she was coming in late because of late-night parties. I feel awful."

"That's OK, Bill, you were too busy to notice. And what about Michael?"

"Well, on the surface everything seemed fine with him. But the more we talked and went over the plans, it became clear that Michael has the workload of about four people and no one seems to be helping him. There's absolutely no way he's going to hit *any* of the deadlines on any of his projects for the next quarter... or even the next half!"

"It turns out that what troubles Michael the most is that he can't see how he'll ever get through those evaluations I told you about yesterday. He seems to really like the people who work for him, but he's just so overwhelmed."

"Gee, Bill, sounds like someone I know!"

"And how about Ronald?"

"Ronald actually is quite the character. The more he talks, the more his brilliance comes through. You know, he still feels bitter about not ever being rewarded for essentially giving birth to Grand View?"

"Ronald also has a pretty good idea of how the company can productize software and get it to market much faster than we do now. Who would have thought that some software engineer would be thinking of such things?"

"It turns out that once I *stopped* I could see that there was a lot more going on than I thought."

Find It

Stop, look, and listen
to understand what is
truly going on

Change It

"Bill, you have made absolutely tremendous progress in only a couple of days. You clearly are ready for step two."

"As you can see, it is critical to *stop* and rationally observe what is going on around you. *Stopping* gives you the ability to calmly see the bigger picture, and to see more holistically. As you now know all too well, things are not always as they appear."

"You can say that again," said Bill.

"It has been said that the path to wisdom goes from data to information to knowledge to wisdom. Most people get bogged down at the data and information stages and never make it to the other side."

"Like when I was only focusing on making the numbers and not observing the situations of the people who work for me," said Bill. "I was sending out plenty of data and information but certainly was lacking any knowledge."

"Right, Bill. The classic definition of knowledge is knowing something gained through experience. Knowledge is simply the condition of being aware."

"Too many people today are just not aware of things, though they may have plenty of data and information. They fail to make the next leap on the road to wisdom. They fail to get the knowledge."

"*Stopping* and *clearly observing* gives you an opportunity to collect enough information to actually find the knowledge."

"Once you have found this knowledge, the second step is to impact the situation for the better."

"So the second stage is to *Change It*. Once you have the knowledge to see the entire situation, you must commit to improve it. You do this by taking concrete steps to improve on what you see and hear."

"The changes to improve the situation can be small. However, each small improvement you cause can, in turn, effect a dramatic improvement in the actions of others around you."

Bill interrupted: "OK, I understand the *stopping* part. But to try to fix everything you see when *stopped*... I mean, that could be a full-time job in itself!"

"That would be an apparent conclusion, but that's not really what happens. As it turns out, many of the things that trouble people are quite easy to fix, once you see and understand them."

"But no matter how small they may seem to the person doing the fixing, they can be very major to the individual who is living with the issue. The reason is, there are different things that stress people and there are different stress points for each person."

"It's no secret that the level of stress at work today is high. There are constant deadlines, increasing customer demands, conflicting responsibilities, and budget constraints."

"Overall employee morale at companies is lower than it used to be. Part of the reason for this is that when companies go through tough economic times, they become more insular."

"When times get tough, the first thing businesses do is tighten their budgets. This means everyone inside the business has fewer resources to get the job done. As a result, there is less time to get done what has to get done, since there are fewer people to do each thing."

"While this is happening, customer demands continue, further stretching the abilities of the people in the business to keep those customers satisfied. The employees who deal with the customers see and feel this the most. Many want to be able to better serve their customers, but their hands become tied. They just don't have enough internal support. They might not have enough staff or permission to hire, or whatever."

"It becomes a downward spiral from there. Executives and managers start to feel more and more pressured to deliver, since the expectations from either shareholders or their bosses on down change, even though the means to achieve those results are gradually decreased."

"People at the top don't get the results they were looking for, so further cuts are made, making it even more difficult for those who are still working to get their jobs done."

Bill was getting the picture.

"It gets worse from there, Bill. Because there are fewer people to do the same amount of work, the employees start to feel oppressed. Even though they really want to do a good job, they aren't allowed to."

"They also see that others they know lost their jobs as part of the cost cutting, so they start to fear they could be next."

"The managers and employees start to feel a lack of loyalty on the part of the company. After all, if they could cut an entire division because of a merger, or eliminate half a department to cut costs, how much do they value each individual?"

"This, in turn, leads to a lack of loyalty to the company on the part of the employee."

"And that, Bill, leads to a lot of stress. You can find it in parts of many companies today."

"People don't generally get stressed because of one thing, though that can happen on occasion. They usually are stressed by a string or series of events or occurrences."

"There was one instance where an employee became absolutely outraged and went screaming and yelling into the office and at her boss because someone had taken her parking space that day."

"Just for taking her parking space?" Bill asked.

"Yes, that's what it looked like, Bill. But what seemed to her boss to be a gross overreaction was actually only the last in a long series of events that set her off. The woman had been working without a vacation for six straight months. No one in management ever thanked her for working over both the Thanksgiving and the Christmas holidays. She was feeling overworked and under appreciated. On top of this, her husband had recently lost his job. The bills were rapidly mounting, and her hot water heater burst the night before, flooding the basement and ruining many of the treasures and the prized clothing in her hope chest. She took a freezing shower before work that day."

"Just as she was about to pull into a parking space, the manager who had just been very publicly praised the day before for a project that this woman actually did most of the work on, cut her off and took the space. She had to drive to the back of the lot to park. That was the last straw."

"The point is, these kinds of stresses can be totally avoided by changes in little things, which you can execute if you *stop* and then *commit*."

"In the case of the woman in the parking situation, her manager was also working long and hard hours. If he had *stopped*, he would have noticed that this employee was working all the time and that she had not had a break in months. He should have publicly thanked her for all her hard work, and especially for volunteering for the holiday duties."

"It is critical today to take time to say thank you. Every day, you should be thanking people around you. This is yet another way to improve a situation around you."

"Even though people working 11-hour days might feel hard-pressed to feel thankful for anything to do with work, if they *stop* and look around they'll see someone who deserves their thanks and that, by itself, improves the situation."

"Working people should thank their families for understanding or at least appreciating how hard they work when not at home. They should thank their spouse or family for working so hard at home while they are at the office, since neither is necessarily easy."

"There are plenty of people you can thank, if you *stop*, see it, and decide to take positive action to improve the situation."

"You should thank the people who worked long hours to get that report or project done, so that you could be more effective at a meeting or even get much-needed sleep. Everyone at work should thank the assistants and secretaries, who make the business work."

"You can thank the person who copied you on that email as well as the one who did not copy you on that useless one."

As Bill listened to Teacher, he started thinking of all those things he never thanked people for. The more he thought, the longer the list grew.

There was the time Bill had promised to pick up Peter after school, but at the last minute asked Jessica to do it because he was so busy at work. She had to miss her art class and he never even thanked her for covering for him.

He never thanked Ted Hopkins for giving him the promotion and later supporting him when things weren't going well.

He didn't thank his assistant Rebecca Johnson for working all those extra hours or the security guard who would lock up after him every night.

Bill was starting to think there were just so many people he hadn't thanked all along his path. He wanted to go back and do it over, but it was too late.

How could I have missed this for so long? Jess and I spent years teaching Peter to say thank you every time he received something from someone. Peter thanks us for things all the time. He even thanks his mom for making dinner.

Maybe we all learn this when we're young and just forget it over time. Or maybe we don't forget, we just don't take the time to say it. Then it moves to the bottom of our mental lists or habits. Or maybe we just get so busy that we forget.

"Thank you, Teacher."

"You are most welcome, Bill."

It was a start.

From that moment forward, Bill decided that he would commit to improving the situation around him. He needed more information from Teacher.

"So, Teacher, tell me more. What else should I do besides looking for signs of stress and saying *thank you* to more people along the way?"

"There is plenty that can be done."

"The what-to-do is actually the easy part. The challenge is making the total commitment to constantly improve everything around you on a regular basis."

"However, if you correctly *stop* and *observe*, what you have to do will become obvious. And once you establish the pattern of observing and acting, it will become very natural for you."

"Eventually, you won't even have to think about it, as it becomes part of the way you are."

"Committing to improve situations, no matter how large or small, will instill a sense of confidence in you by those around you. The top things that improve employee loyalty are confidence in leadership and trust."

"People want to believe in the people they work for. When they see you constantly striving to improve what's around you, it increases their confidence in you. They will know you are trying to do the right thing, not for yourself, but for others. This leads to a sense of trust and, if widespread, can become part of a company's culture."

"By their actions, too many companies tell their employees they don't care about them. It might be lack of a career path, passed over promotions, cold-hearted layoffs, or compensation or pay raises that fail to match performance."

"One of the worst things a company can do is to give everyone the same percentage pay increase. The people working the hardest — and those not — all see this. When all of them are compensated the same, those working the hardest essentially are told they shouldn't put forth so much effort and those who are not working at one hundred percent are told they don't have to work any harder. This kind of message from management makes it difficult to recruit and keep really good people."

"So Teacher, a lot of it is about the money!"

"No, it's not really about the money, per se, Bill. However, compensation is one of the true statements an executive, a manager, or even a company makes about his or her employees. Compensation is only one official, quantitative statement by the company as to how it values each person's contribution to the organization."

"People at work today don't just want more money. They want to grow. They want more knowledge, more training, and more opportunity. They want to be empowered. They want things delegated to them. They also want more balance in their lives."

"Employees want to be treated well. Remember, a large percent of a person's life is spent at work. If that time is made just a little more pleasant, it will increase morale, one person at a time."

"That then leads to more confidence in the people who the employees work for. Ultimately, this leads to less stress."

"Sounds logical, sir, but this sounds like a company has to go through a revolution. You're talking about how people get rewarded for what they do, how they get treated, and how they are trained. This could be a big change for some!"

"Well, Bill, it may seem like a big deal but it really isn't, as long as each person does his or her part, which we'll talk about in the third lesson, but that's a bit later."

"Let's take the case of your three employees."

"You said that Stephanie was coming in late frequently because she takes her daughter to the hospital for chemotherapy treatments, right?"

"Yes, several times a month."

"And is everyone on the same time schedule in your group?"

"Not exactly. Some of the programmers work later shifts, coming in later than, say, the general support staff."

"So, you're saying that there is some flexibility in schedules here."

"Definitely."

"Rather than have Stephanie come in late, why not modify her work schedule to accommodate her situation?"

"But Teacher, she comes in late on those days anyway and gets away with it."

"Bill, people in general do not want to get away with something. They only do that as a last resort, because they are in rigid situations and their required needs — in the case of Stephanie, taking her daughter to the hospital—are not being met by the situation."

"What about letting Stephanie work at home at times? Changing Stephanie's schedule will cost you nothing, and she will feel more legitimate in using the time with her daughter, which is time that she needs anyway."

"Because what she is doing becomes legitimized by the company, she can be more productive."

"You end up with a more productive, and no doubt happier, individual."

"So, Teacher, all we have to do is modify Stephanie's schedule? Just let her work at home parts of some days? That's it?"

"I told you earlier that some of the changes that can dramatically improve a situation are small. Changing Stephanie's schedule may seem small to you, but I assure you, it will be a big deal to her!"

"Now what about Michael? What is his situation?"

"Basically, he has way too much to do and can't get to the evaluations that have been bugging him for some time."

"Right. That one's easy as well. You obviously need to lighten his load. Then again, what troubles him most is that he can't get to the evaluations of his staff."

"How many evaluations does he have to do?"

"Probably 13, including his assistant."

"And he plans to meet with each person individually, right?"

"Yes."

"Does he have a strong number two?"

"Yes, that would be Jim Parenti. He's been here almost as long as Michael and knows that area inside out."

"How about talking to Michael about having Jim take over some of Michael's projects for a week, freeing Michael to do the evaluations? He could make Jim the 'Michael-of-thc-Week,' freeing Michael to do all the evaluations."

"There will be three benefits do this. First, Michael gets the evaluations done, eliminating the plaguing issue that troubles him most. Second, it will force Michael to detach himself from the day-to-day grind, much like you did the first day you *stopped.*

"And third, Jim will get a chance to show what he can do."

"In general, people can rise to a level of performance higher than they live at every day. Unfortunately, many are never given the chance. It's not so much that anyone is against giving someone else a new opportunity, they just don't always think about it."

Bill started thinking.

They don't stop and that's why they don't give anyone a chance. They don't see it and it's right in front of them. More people need to stop in order to see this. If they only stopped being so fanatically busy for just a few minutes, they'd see this. But I never saw it! I never stopped either.

I wonder if I missed giving someone else a chance along the way. I must have. I'm sure I have. I never stopped to even see it. I wonder if I prevented anyone from a missed opportunity that damaged his or her career. I sure hope not. I need to be on the lookout for these opportunities for other people.

That's what I'm going to do, commit to watch for opportunities where people can be given a shot at them. I'm going to look for occasions that will cause someone to rise to it and, somehow, get that person matched with that opportunity. And I will give them the tools, training, and support they require. I'm going to give more people a chance!

Teacher continued. "Many people at work also tend to stay in the same job much longer than they should. The reason is simple: it becomes comfortable. Change is difficult."

"For example, if you ever watch an executive telling a group of managers that something is going to be changing in their organization, you can see people get defensive. They fold their arms, almost immediately.

"Then, if the executive identifies one area that will not be changing, the people associated with that area instantly open up and are all for supporting the change."

"People tend to defend why things should stay the way they are and easily find reasons that the new way, whatever it is, won't work. That's human nature."

"The truth is, most people generally are in favor of change, as long as it doesn't affect them and what they do. Their view is that change is great, as long as it's in somebody else's backyard."

"That's why people should change jobs or responsibilities more frequently than they do. A new job or a new task energizes people. Interestingly, the same set of tasks that can be very stale and routine to one person who has done them for a long time can be refreshing and invigorating to another person just starting them."

"So what you'll be doing here is giving both Michael and Jim a taste of change, without all the baggage. In both cases, it's only for a week, so there's not much to lose."

"Yes, Teacher, but much to gain!"

"Precisely. What they will experience is the way it *could* be, which we hope and expect will be a positive experience."

"And Teacher, you know what else?"

"What's that, Bill?"

"This is another case of doing something relatively small on my part that could be very big on both Michael and Jim's part."

"You learn well, Bill. You're going to go far here!"

"Thank you."

"OK, Bill, what about Ronald. You mentioned that he was, I think you said brilliant, but a bit unhappy with the company. What do you think should be done to improve that situation?"

"Thought you'd never ask! I have two ideas. First, I think we should have an office event, a party, or something where we officially, as UniShare, thank Ronald for essentially creating the product that launched Grand View. Secondly, there's a monthly meeting where all the divisions report and discuss company wide issues. I think we should send Ronald to those to represent us."

"Why, Bill?"

"Well, since he doesn't like some of the things that come from Corporate, this would give him a chance to speak out at the source. Also, he just might be right about some of the edicts that come from across the river, so he might improve the situation for everyone."

"This also will let others see how smart this guy really is."

"Anyway, those are my two ideas. What do you think?"

"Very nice, Bill. You *stopped* to understand the issues and have come up with a very fine solution to improve that situation. You just have to follow through on those commitments, which is really important."

"You see, there's *stopping, seeing, understanding, committing to improvement,* and then there is the all-important *follow-through,* the actual execution of that commitment to improvement."

"Is that the toughest part, Teacher?"

"The toughest part is stopping and moving into this mode of identification and improvement. But once you make the change, you don't go back. Once you start behaving in the ways we've been discussing, more positive habits form. You start to see things around you in a different way, and not just at work."

Bill remembered the smile on his son's face the day before when Bill surprised him at the bus stop. Teacher was right. Sometimes it is a very small thing that can bring joy to someone else.

That night over dinner, Bill talked to Jessica and Peter about his day. They could tell he was excited. He was feeling so accomplished and, for the first time in a long time, he was energized about work.

It no longer was about the physical and mental labor. Now it was about making everything he touched a bit better. It was like heavy weights had been removed from his shoulders.

Bill asked Jessica and Peter about their day and listened intently. Jessica was having a tough time with one of her art classes, having to complete an assignment in the fine art of self-portraits, her least favorite part.

Bill suggested that she ask her teacher for some extra help after class next week and he offered to leave work early to pick up Peter. He could spend the rest of the afternoon with Peter, then work at home in the evening.

The next day, Bill got into work by 7:30 a.m., feeling very positive and ready to take on the world.

Teacher was waiting for him at his office.

"Well, good morning Teacher. Did you sleep here? "

"No, I just got here Bill."

"Luna's?"

"Yes, Bill, and thanks for offering."

What the heck, these coffee breaks have been pretty enlightening so far, Bill thought.

Over coffee, Bill wondered what the last lesson was. He hoped it would at least have something to do with making the numbers, since Bill knew that would still be in front of him when finished this round of *stopping*.

He also wondered how to integrate the *stopping* and the re-starting, and how long he should stay *stopped* for.

Teacher seemed to sense Bill's questions in advance.

"So Bill, by now you're probably wondering when and how the actual work will get done if you're *stopped* all the time, right?"

"You hit it on the head Teacher. Corporate still has high expectations of this division. After all, it is a new acquisition that UniShare wants not only to be proud of, but based on the sales and revenue projections we agreed to, they also want it to be successful."

"OK, Bill. Let's talk again about the *stopping* and *committing* for a minute."

"The fundamental problem that *stopping* solves is lack of awareness. When people have their heads down all the time, they may not always be aware of what is going on. They lose a sense of context."

"*Stopping* is not a permanent state. *Stopping* can be for a minute or a day. The amount of time doesn't matter as much as the act of awareness; seeing what needs to be seen."

"The more you *stop*, *look*, and *understand*, the more intuitive it becomes and the less time it takes. The point is to consciously detach yourself from what is causing all your focus during a period of time so you can look up."

"So, Teacher, you don't totally walk away from work all together for a great period of time by *stopping*?"

"Here's another way to look at it."

"The amount of time you spend actually *stopped*, or the total time that you are not technically working on whatever you were working on, will be replaced by other benefits resulting from your actions in changing things for the better."

"You can't see what needs to be done to make something better without *stopping* to see it."

"This is why vacations without connections to the office are so important. People need to break away from work to mentally recharge. It's very healthy."

Change It

Commit to improve the situation
by taking concrete steps to improve
what you see and hear

Pass It On

"If you think about it, Bill, when you find the knowledge that allows you to change the situation for the better, it can only lead to positive results. And that's where making the numbers comes in."

Oh, finally! Here comes the secret of making the numbers. This must be the third lesson. It must have to do with getting everyone to work harder. After all, if I'm stopped for some periods of time, others are going to have to pick up the slack.

Then again, there really hasn't been any extra time around here that I can see. How can anyone work any harder? On the other hand, the first two steps I learned have worked for me already, so the third should work too. Whatever it is.

"OK, Bill, I think you are you ready for the third and most important lesson of the three."

"Yes, please tell me!"

"The third lesson is to *Pass It On.*"

"You must clearly communicate your new knowledge and commitment to improvement to those around you."

"You have to get as many people around you as possible to *stop* and *find it*, commit to *change it* and then have them get others to do the same."

"It is not usually one big thing that bogs people down in a department or in a company. It is generally what seems like a thousand little things."

"This is why *passing it on* is so important. No one person can find and fix everything, there are too many things to fix."

"So, you mean I need to get Stephanie, Michael, and Ronald to *stop* and observe to truly understand the situation around them, then commit to improvement? And then motivate them to *pass it on* to others?"

"Yes, Bill. As a result, more issues will get addressed and more people will have a positive impact on those around them."

"The more people who *find it, change it,* and *pass it on,* the more the overall situation will improve."

"Now that makes a lot of sense, Teacher! But what about productivity? We still have some tough hills to climb here."

"Well, the first step is to determine what should be eliminated from what is already being done."

"I don't totally understand, Teacher."

"Think of it this way. When people work in a particular place for a period of time, they create processes, or ways that they work. This is very natural."

"However, after more and more time, the situation can change, even though those original ways of doing things don't."

"People think in terms of starting new things, not stopping old things. It is much easier to start something than it is to stop it. Just think for a minute. I'm sure you can think of at least one thing you know you should stop."

Let's see. There's that edict I issued my first week for all managers to detail every five days the status of every project they are working on.

Then there's that Wednesday update meeting, where everyone reports on his or her progress. That meeting's getting close to two hours now. Maybe that reporting can be done less frequently, or even by email. Everyone at that meeting tries to say more than the previous person so they can look like they're doing as much or more than the next person. Maybe that's why that meeting is out of control.

It's my fault. I can stop letting people talk longer and longer. We should reduce the length of the meetings, if nothing else.

"Yes, Teacher, there's probably something I can stop."

"This is where an increase in efficiency comes in. As a leader, you can guide what is looked for when people are in *stop* mode. For example, once people learn to *stop*, *look,* and *listen* well, they can be asked to carefully look around and identify those things that should be stopped."

"It might be a regular staff meeting that has always been held. Perhaps some people who attend other meetings don't need to be there. Perhaps certain other meetings shouldn't be held at all."

"Maybe a regular report that is issued is not needed anymore. Stopping that will save time for the report writer as well as those who receive and read it. This may sound small, but even if a report is not necessary for someone, they still have to determine that when they receive it. It takes time to make that assessment, even if it's a quick decision."

"So getting people to *stop* and then to stop things they can identify around them is one of several categories where you can lead by creating a focus?"

"Yes. When you get others around you to *stop* and commit to improvement around them, there is a cascading effect. The atmosphere changes. People start looking for better ways to do things."

"As better ways to do things are found, personal performance improves and efficiency increases."

"What you find, Bill, is that if you can get people to *stop* and *find it*, and truly commit to *change it*, they will be able to separate what matters from what doesn't."

"As you have discovered, when people get too caught up in what they're doing minute-by-minute, day-by-day, and week-by-week, they lose perspective."

"There's a workaholic adage of 'if we just get this done, then we can go have some fun.' But it never gets done."

"Many people live like that, but they don't always realize it."

"This is why *passing it on* is so important. One person can make a difference. Two people can make a bigger difference. An entire group of people can make a monumental difference."

"Margaret Mead, the noted anthropologist, once said something like 'never doubt that a small group of thoughtful, committed individuals can change the world. Indeed, it is the only thing that ever has.'"

"Again, Bill, it's not that one major thing changes, it's about many, many things changing for the better in many people's lives."

"Just like you made some small changes for Stephanie, Michael, and Ronald, they, in turn, can create some positive changes in others around them."

"*Passing it on* requires sharing information and knowledge with others."

"That, in turn, makes a person more selfless and less self-preoccupied and more focused on improving situations."

"Once there is more selflessness in a group, department, or organization, people can focus more on doing things better."

"People then become much more attuned to activities and situations around them. They also start looking out for one another, as each person looks for ways to improve someone else's situation. It creates a sense of cooperation and even team-building of sorts."

"Yes, Teacher, I think I get it. What you're saying is that if I'm watching out for someone else, and they're watching out for someone else, things will work out."

"And I don't really have to focus on myself because ultimately others will also be looking out for me, as long as I pass along these lessons and others pass it along as well."

"So, once we *pass it on* to enough people in my department, the department should run better, because so many people will be *stopping*, looking for improvements around them, and then committing themselves to make those improvements.

"Yes, Bill, that's it. The result is a team effort at getting things done. This leads to much greater efficiency because people identify tasks that can be eliminated or reduced, as they understand the bigger picture. Then the concept of making the numbers becomes much easier, because there is less waste and more focus on what needs to be done."

"You also have people on the lookout for situations they might improve. People also feel better, which is only natural as they assist others."

"*Passing it on* also helps many to get out of ruts they didn't realize they were in."

"I sure can relate to that, Teacher. I thought the way to get more done was to work more hours. What I now see is that I was increasing the number of hours I worked, but the amount of what I was getting done was decreasing. It probably would have gotten even worse. Thank you, Teacher."

"You're welcome Bill. Now, how about you get to work and *pass it on* to your team. I'll check back with you later, just to see how things are going."

This is great. I now have a way to help the people in my department to do better. I wonder if I should tell everyone at the same time or one at a time? I'll start with Stephanie, Michael, and Ronald. Yes, that's it. I'll start with them.

What if they don't get it? Or worse, what if they don't buy in? Michael is so busy he may not even want to take the time to talk about it. But then again, he did get all his evaluations done, so he lived through the result, even though he doesn't yet know it.

Bill called Stephanie, Michael, and Ronald and asked them all to meet for coffee at Luna's at 8 the next morning. He told them he had something very important he wanted to discuss.

Over coffee (and tea for Ronald), Bill started to describe the epiphany of sorts he had over the last few weeks. He was totally candid with the trio. He told them that he had been feeling very distressed that he and his department would not deliver to Corporate what he had agreed to. He recounted how he didn't know what he was going to do, other than try to work more hours and get everyone else to do the same. He had been losing hope, was hardly seeing his family, and just wasn't happy.

Bill confided that he had felt that he had gotten in over his head at work and was feeling anxious that there was no way out.

He told them of how he had learned some new and significant lessons from a person Corporate had sent to help him. He described what a difference a few changes in his life had made in his work habits, his attitude, and approach to work, and even his home life.

The three listened intently, all personally relating to the over-worked part.

Bill *stopped* and listened for the group's reaction.

Michael was the first to speak.

"Well, Bill, I'm not sure exactly what you learned, but if it has anything to do with you coming up with the idea of giving me time to do those evaluations, then it's a very good thing."

Since Bill had been so forthcoming, Michael felt he would do the same.

"You may not know this, but I felt that those evaluations were hanging over my head, day and night. I felt I was cheating the people who worked for me, delaying their raises, because the evaluations weren't done. No one ever said anything, but it was just eating away at me inside. By freeing time for me to get to the evaluations, you relieved me of that stress. And it was a great opportunity for Jim."

"Here, here," said Ronald. "By giving Jim a chance to do Mike's job for a bit, he got a better feel for how much this guy actually does. Jim told me later that he loved it! He said he found it exciting to have that many projects going simultaneously."

"And for me," Ronald continued, "you made a big change in my life here just by that office party you threw for me. It really meant a lot and I'll never forget it."

"Not to mention the meetings I now attend at Corporate. You know, some of those guys are a lot smarter than I thought."

"They don't always pass enough information along for us all to see what they really mean. However, when I told them that at the meeting, they all listened, discussed it, and agreed to try to do better. I was quite impressed."

Stephanie had been the quietest of the group. But after Michael and Ronald spoke, they very naturally looked to Stephanie for her comments.

"Well, my situation is a bit different. You all know that my daughter has been sick and I've needed extra time for her treatments. Allowing me to work at home a few days a month has made all the difference in the world to me, Bill. So whatever you were told to do, please keep doing it."

"Thank you all for being so open."

They did notice! Teacher was right. I thought these were small, insignificant changes for each of these people, but to these people it's apparent that they were huge. Their lives were positively affected. I never would have imagined. If I can get them to do the same thing for their subordinates, well, this could be very, very big.

"That's really why we're here, gang. I want to pass on to each of you the lessons I have learned and see if we might collectively follow the same simple steps to make even more improvements around all of us."

"The first thing we all need to do is *stop* and take time to *look* and *listen* to understand what is going on in each of our immediate areas. This allows you to *find it*, the 'it' being the knowledge of what is truly going on around you. What I found out by *stopping* is that things are not always as they appear."

"Michael, when I *stopped* and *listened*, it became obvious to me that those evaluations were really bugging you. I also found that your workload was very large."

"Ronald, when I *stopped* I came to realize that the organization never appropriately thanked you for your great initial contribution. It also was apparent that you had, shall we say, a slight disdain for some of the wisdom at Corporate."

They all laughed.

"And Stephanie, well, I found that you needed more flexibility in personal time, which is totally understandable."

"The point is that these situations were all there for some time and I never saw them. For that, I want to apologize to all of you. I'm sorry I didn't see any of these situations sooner."

"But you see, by *stopping*, I found the knowledge that made each of these situations obvious."

"Finding the knowledge of the situation around you is the first step. The second lesson is to *change it*, that is, to commit to improve the situation that you recognize by *stopping*."

"You each experienced the result of my trying to change your situations for the better based on the knowledge I found when I *stopped*."

"Michael, you clearly needed a break from your regular workload if you were ever going to get the evaluations done. By having Jim take over that load for a bit, you could get the evaluations completed, thereby taking a load off your shoulders."

"Ironically, Bill, you *stopping* actually caused me to *stop*," said Michael.

"How do you mean?"

"Well, when you took my daily workload away for a bit, it was so much easier to focus on the evaluations. For some reason, they were easier to do and my one-on-one meetings with the employees were very focused. I guess there was nothing else in the way."

"Great observation, Michael."

"And Bill, I think I *stopped* for a while at that meeting at Corporate," Ronald interjected. "I mean, I was removed from my day-to-day wheel-spinning, even if only for a few moments. During that meeting I was totally focused on looking at the bigger picture of what would make things better. In that case, it was getting others to communicate more clearly."

"And Stephanie, by working at home a few days, my guess is that you've had more time to actually think."

"That's absolutely right, Bill. It turns out that by eliminating a few trips to and from the office, I actually ended up with more time for work, with fewer distractions. And it gave me more quality time with my daughter."

"So, you each, in a way, have had a taste of *stopping*. But you were on the receiving end in these cases. Now we need to turn that around so that you can consciously *stop, look,* and *listen* and see what areas around you can be improved.

Then it's important to commit to taking concrete steps to improve what you see."

"But Bill, we're all pretty buried, as you well know, as you found when you *stopped* and looked," said Michael.

"Yes, everyone at work is very busy. What we all have to do, though, is increase our sense of observations and identify how we can all become much more efficient and productive."

"For example, one thing I am committing to do is shorten all the meetings I run, as well as put a top meeting time limit of one hour."

"Hey, I just picked up about three hours a week," said Ronald.

"We *all* did," said Stephanie.

Everyone laughed.

"This all sounds very positive," Ronald said. "Is there anything else?"

"Yes, there's one more thing. After you *find it* and *change it*, you must also commit to p*ass it on.* That is, to share these lessons in the same way that I am sharing with you."

"You can *pass it on* in to your subordinates in the best way you choose. Everyone is different."

"But this is just the beginning of the process. It's not about *stopping* one time, taking stock, and fixing something. It's about changing many of our habits and behaviors so that we each regularly look around and assess the situation with proper perspective."

"I hope and expect that this will lead to continuous improvement throughout the department."

"This may sound corny, but improving things for other people makes you feel good. At least it does for me."

"You know, I actually followed some of this at home and it even made a big difference there. For several months, I had been at home but not really there, if you know what I mean."

"I wasn't paying enough attention. I found that *stopping, listening,* and *deciding* to make things better works anywhere, once you get into the habit. Maybe it's easier for some than others, I don't know."

"Now that you mention it, Bill, you have seemed happier at the office lately," said Ronald. "You used to come in and we wouldn't see you for hours at a time. I, for one, was surprised to see you at my office and even asking me questions about what I was up to. It gave me the sense that you were starting to care about me."

"I wouldn't go that far." Bill and the trio all laughed.

"OK, Bill, how do we start?" asked Michael. "What do we do?"

"How about spending the morning just checking around your department. Talk to people. See what's on their minds. And look for at least one thing to *stop*. After all, we have to pick up time somewhere if we're going to *stop* and take time to change things for the better."

"How about we regroup in the conference room after lunchtime."

As he did so many times recently, Bill left Luna's for the short walk to the office, this time in a quartet. He wondered what Teacher was doing that morning.

As Bill had suggested, Michael, Stephanie, and Ronald dropped their things in their offices and went out to mingle with the troops.

As Michael walked around, he thought back to the meetings he had recently conducted with each of his staffers during the evaluation process.

Who seemed most troubled? What did I miss? What was someone trying to tell me that I didn't hear? Was everybody happy? Did anyone mention that they liked working here? Or working for me? Did I ask the right questions?

After thinking for a while, Michael went directly to see Robert Manero. Michael remembered how Bob said he could handle more responsibility.

"Hey, Bob, what's going on?"

"Not too much, Mike. And you?"

"I was thinking about how you said the other day that you could handle more to do. Did you mean it?"

"Yes, absolutely. I didn't think you'd remember. I mean, you're so busy and all."

"Here's an idea, Bob. You're very familiar with how we do things around here. How about you take a few moments and jot down some ideas on how we might do things better. For example, is there a more efficient way to work or deal with our customers or suppliers? Or how could we improve how we work internally? Anything like that."

"Sure, Mike, I'd be happy to take a crack at that. Thanks for the opportunity. I'll get something to you in about a week, if that's OK."

"That would be great, Bob. Thanks."

A little later, as he continued speaking with other employees, Michael passed Bob in the hallway. He couldn't help but notice a new energy in Bob that hadn't observed before, as if he was really charged and on a mission. He wondered if it had something to do with his earlier talk with him.

Ronald spoke with the people in his group, which included the unlikely mix of computer programmers and business development folks. The more Ronald went back and forth between the two types, the more he realized how different they were from one another.

The group had grown together from the beginning. It had started as a software programming focus. As the company grew, more programmers were added, and put under Ronald's management. Ronald was highly creative and everyone knew he was the go-to person to get through any development bottlenecks.

In its early years, the company's innovation and new products almost always came out of Ronald's group. It only seemed logical, at the time, that the function of creating new business would fall there.

Over time, Ronald found that creating new business and keeping current customers happy would sometimes conflict. He often found himself going back and forth between both camps, trying to balance the desires of Corporate to have a flow of new products and the customers, who were more concerned with getting the most out of the products they already had.

As Ronald sat down and listened to more of his subordinates, he realized something significant had to be changed. He had come up with an idea that he thought might dramatically change his entire group for the better. He couldn't wait for the afternoon meeting.

Stephanie, always considered *the efficient one* by her peers, briefly met with many of her staff members. One person gave her his opinion and some ideas on the budgeting process for the company and another told her he was getting tired of working so many hours and so many days in a row. Stephanie listened carefully and took it all in.

As the group gathered in the conference room to meet with Bill, everyone seemed enthusiastic and excited. They all wanted to share what they had learned.

Michael started. "From what I heard from my folks, we have some people who are overworked while others are looking for new challenges and opportunities. Looks like we have an imbalance of workload. The good news is, several people are looking for more to do."

"Let me correct that slightly. People aren't necessarily looking for more to do; they're looking for more responsibility and more challenge."

I never noticed that in my group. I guess I might have underestimated some of these people. And here I thought I had to do everything. Some of these people are probably up to doing some of the things that I thought only I could do. How naïve of me! I overburden myself while people are looking for more to do. And I've totally missed those overworked people. Well, that stops now. All we have to do is balance this more.

"So, Michael, what do you propose?"

"Well, Bill, it looks like we should give more responsibility and challenge to some, and reduce some of the workload on those who are over-burdened. Seems obvious once you *stop* and look at it."

"There's one person in particular, Jim Parenti, who looks like he's ready to take on greater responsibility. Perhaps we should consider moving him up."

"Great idea, Michael. How do you feel Jim did handling your tasks for that week that you worked on the evaluation?"

"He did a great job. I think he's ready for more responsibility. Maybe he could become my number two, if you're comfortable with that?"

"That would be fine."

"OK, Ronald, any observations on your side?"

"Yes, one that could be a very big one. I know we were just supposed to listen to people and gain knowledge that might make some things better. But the more I listened to the people in my group, the more I came to realize there is a significant conflict in what we're asking people to do."

"On one hand, we're asking the business development people to concentrate on creating new products. On the other hand, we ask the support staff and programmers to support the sales staff and customers with the products we sell now."

"Since both these types of people work together, they often get sucked into each other's area, to the detriment of their own."

"Maybe we should split the two into separate groups and let each focus on their specific areas."

"That's a tremendous idea," said Stephanie. "That can tie directly into some of what I learned. We have one person who suggested we link the budgeting process much closer to product development, so that we might more accurately plan what is going to be coming out of development."

"It turns out that although Ronald's group is obviously very involved in the planning process, there is a heavy emphasis on the second group Ronald mentioned, the programming types."

"The good news is that those adjustments usually are on the positive side, since we didn't plan well enough to know how the new products might do."

"However, the down side is that the budgets are being created with a false sense of what our business is for the coming year."

"Yes, Stephanie, good observation," said Ronald. "We end up introducing new products into the marketplace and when we do we're really just guessing how well they'll do. Product development and budgets aren't linked tightly enough. And there's more."

"I mean, some of the planning people said they don't spend much time with customers on what the future customer needs might be. As a result, they feel we develop some products that either never make it to market or don't do well once we launch them."

"Even worse," said Ronald, "the development people don't feel a sense of responsibility, which they say they want."

"That's one of the reasons we have to keep adjusting the budgets. But even worse, people work on things that, in their minds, are destined to fail or not do as well as they might have. They feel they are wasting time. By fixing that, we can pick up a significant amount of time and work on products that have a better chance of success."

"And in the process, we can provide more challenge and opportunity for the people and get them focused on working on things that matter."

"Great ideas, Ronald. Thank you. And thank you all."

"So what do we do now?"

"We commit and execute all these ideas," said Michael.

"And then we need to *pass it on*, so everyone can start improving things around them," said Stephanie.

"OK, let's get to it," Bill said. "Feel free to keep me posted on progress as you share the lessons with those around you."

After a few more hours of work, Bill started heading home.

That went even better than I had hoped. Mike, Stephanie, and Ronald seemed to really get it. I can't believe how much they recognized in each of their areas in such a short period of time. I guess just taking the time to stop and look is all it sometimes takes. And coming up with a solution to the problem. Yes, that's pretty key, too. I wonder if they'll follow through on each of the ideas. If they do, their jobs should each get a little easier. Their staffs should get a lot out of this too. I can't remember seeing Mike, Stephanie, and Ronald this energized.

The idea that Michael would even consider giving up some of his responsibilities; now that's major! And Stephanie linking her findings with Ronald's. Very nice. This might lead to more internal cooperation.

Maybe as people look at improving things for others around them, they become more drawn to the bigger picture. I wonder. I'll have to ask Teacher about this.

I wonder if we can keep this up? After I get back to the realities of getting my job done on a day-to-day basis, I wonder if I'll continue to find it and *change it. I wonder if I'll continue to stop on a regular basis. Guess we'll have to see.*

After dinner, Bill told Jessica about the third lesson of *passing it on* that he had learned. He explained how he *passed it on* to his three key people and how effectively and quickly they understood and put it into practice.

Bill also mentioned the positive reactions he saw in Michael, Stephanie, and Ronald and told Jessica how it seemed to give them all more energy and a positive approach to change things around them for the better.

Not only was Jessica paying close attention, she was thinking how she might apply some of these lessons in her own life.

Meanwhile, several towns away, Michael was putting into practice at home what he had learned at work. He hadn't planned it that way, it just happened naturally. Mike's wife, Theresa, who worked at a local branch of a very large bank, was talking about her day.

Mike had heard the story before. Everyone, it seems, has been commiserating with each other about how bad the branch manager treats everyone who works there. Theresa had spoken about it many times, but Mike didn't have any solid advice to offer.

Theresa talked about how the manager made people work overtime at the last minute, giving no consideration for any personal plans they might have. She described how he didn't even allow a small Friday afternoon office party after closing to celebrate a co-worker's new engagement.

It wasn't that the manager was a bad guy, he actually was kind of fun. Outside of work, he was very approachable. Everyone at the office just thought he took work too seriously and worked so hard that he didn't notice events around him and how his actions were affecting the team.

Theresa explained how the manager had no idea that one employee's distraught father had recently come to live with him following his mother's recent passing. The branch manager was the only one from the small office who didn't pay his respects or even send flowers. He was working that day.

"All he does is work," said Theresa. "He doesn't seem to care about anyone."

Michael thought for a moment and decided to *pass it on* to his wife, since the manager seemed like such a candidate to be *stopped.*

After Michael explained the three lessons to Theresa and the immediate and amazing results he witnessed at work that day, Theresa wanted to know more. She wanted to know how to let the branch manager in on this, and how to make him *stop* to realize the situation around him.

Michael suggested she just relay to the manager what Michael had relayed to her. Michael suggested she tell the manager what was happening at UniShare and the success her husband's department was experiencing just by a few people *stopping.*

Theresa figured she had nothing to lose and decided she would talk to the manager the next day.

The next few weeks at Bill's division the office seemed to come alive. Bill would pass two people laughing together in the hallway and another person would go by humming. And it wasn't just the people who were humming. The business started taking off as well.

Passing by one office, Bill stopped in his tracks. There in the middle of an employee's office was a five-foot, obviously homemade *stop* sign. It had a Styrofoam base, with a modified broom handle coming out of the center. At the top of the pole was the familiar octagon *stop* sign. The front was a bright red STOP. The back of the sign simply had the words *Pass It On.*

A group of employees had decided that the best way to make sure the lessons were not forgotten was to create a portable sign that anyone could *deliver* anonymously to any employee or manager they felt was getting out of touch and not in tune with events around them.

"Hi there. A gift?"

"Oh, hi Bill," said the employee. "Yes, I got the message. He chuckled."

The next morning, Bill noticed the sign sitting near the reception area, available to anyone who might need it. Someone had even made a green cover for the *stop* sign, with the UniShare logo in the center.

From that day on, every employee would look as they passed the reception desk to see if the sign was there. Some days it would be sitting there, with the green, 'all-signals-go' cover. Other days, it would be missing, but everyone knew it was being put to good use.

Even when the stop sign was found in a person's office, that person took it as a positive gesture of support from colleagues. It was a quick, "hey, take-a-break" signal.

Bill was at headquarters several days later to attend a company-wide presentation. After the meeting, he bumped into Mark Jordan, the senior vice president who had introduced Bill to his team just after UniShare acquired Grand View.

"Bill, how are you? How is everything?"

"Oh, hello. Things are going very well, thank you. Do you have a few minutes? I'd like to ask you something."

"Sure. Come on in. What's on your mind, Bill?"

"I have a question. It's about Teacher. How did the company find this guy?"

"Why do you ask? Was he helpful?"

"That would be an understatement. He was incredibly helpful. I mean, to the point of changing everything. Dramatically. For the better."

"Glad he could be of some help. Now about your question. You probably know a little of the history of UniShare, right?"

"Well, just that it was founded a long time ago by a man who had a lot of ideas and, according to legend, was somewhat of a recluse."

"It was something like that, Bill. The man's name was Ryan Dakota (RD) Ridgeway. He was very creative and had a way with people. He used to share all his ideas from the time he started the company and he encouraged everyone to share theirs as well."

"Some people couldn't get used to the idea of being so open around their peers. Mr. Ridgeway found over time that those kinds of people didn't seem to stay with the company very long, even though some of them were very smart."

"So over the years, Mr. Ridgeway started to have the executives focus on hiring and developing the kind of people who might be more open to sharing with one another, so that everyone could use the best practices that were developed company wide."

"His theory was that if people were sharing, the work environment would be more open. He also reasoned that sharing would require an increase in communication. He felt that if more work issues were openly discussed, there would be less wasted time on something that everyone thought was a bad idea. He also thought that in this kind of a work environment, there would more autonomy and challenge, which he firmly believed individuals want above all else, even money."

"Mr. Ridgeway figured that with that kind of an environment for everyone who worked there, the business would very naturally follow. He also wanted his managers and employees to have a healthy balance between their work and home life. He found that if someone spends all his or her time working, they lose perspective."

"He found that when people are balanced, they make better decisions. So he built into the culture at UniShare that balance in one's life was a good thing and should be encouraged."

"It turned out to be quite the formula for success. The company has grown every year since it was started decades ago. There has never been a layoff and once people stay here for a period of time, they tend to stay for a very long time."

"Oh, and as an aside, Mr. Ridgeway became fabulously wealthy. He now spends most of his time on charitable causes and other personal issues that interest him."

"So that explains why no one ever mentions him or sees him at big company meetings. I guess the recluse part is true?"

"Well, let's just say that Mr. Ridgeway likes to maintain a very low profile. Besides, he doesn't really need to work here any more, other than on his pet projects. He pretty much leaves us alone at headquarters."

"His idea with UniShare was to create a company where people want to work."

"I get it," said Bill. "When I researched the company before coming here, I kept hearing about UniShare's positive reputation. That explains it."

"Yes, Bill, we're quite proud of the company reputation, built over a number of years."

"So, what about Teacher?"

"Well, Mr. Ridgeway came up with that idea. He thought if a position of The Teacher was created, the legacy could live on at UniShare. Everyone at Corporate gets it, but with the speed that we're growing, it required that someone go out and spend time passing on the lessons to the new folks. That was the objective in sending Teacher across the river to you. Seems it paid off!"

"Oh, yes, in many ways. The atmosphere at the office is positive. Managers and employees are working together to find ways to do things better. I've never seen anything like it."

"The team has eliminated all kinds of things we all were doing that just wasted time. No one seems to be killing themselves any more, though everyone is working hard. But people feel challenged, and they're all rising to the challenge."

"We've made so many changes, some so small they're not even worth mentioning. But the suggestions are coming from everyone, and each suggestion makes something better. As a result, people are happier."

"What's interesting is that we found that when the employees are happy, it comes through when they deal with our customers. As a result, I keep hearing that our customers like dealing with our people."

"And they're not saying that just because of our products. They're saying it because of the attitude of our people."

"Bill, that is absolutely great news. Thank you so much for sharing it with me."

"Well, I wanted to thank you for the opportunity to do the job and especially for sending Teacher to me."

"Before I go, aren't you going to ask me about how we're doing at making the numbers?"

"Bill, we've found over many years that if all those things that I discussed come to pass, then the numbers follow. Just focusing on making the numbers doesn't accomplish any of the much larger goals we have in mind. When we hit those goals, we generally always make the numbers. Pressuring you or anyone else on increasing sales or revenue without providing you with a reasonable way to do it would be irresponsible on our part."

"Thank you again. Guess I'd better get back across the river to the team."

"Thanks for dropping by, Bill. Come in any time."

During his short drive back the office, Bill thought about his conversation.

That explains a lot. The company actually went out of its way to hire someone to teach these lessons to the new people. Now that's forward thinking. And that's why Corporate wasn't bugging me on making the numbers. They were looking at the bigger picture. They don't just want numbers for the next quarter. That would be too short-term in their thinking.

They want a system in place so they never have to worry about the numbers. That's why they hired Teacher. When he got hired, I hope Teacher asked to be paid based on his success rate. I hope he gets a percentage of the improvement he causes the company. He deserves it!

It was near the end of the day when Bill got back to the office. He was just going to stop in to make sure everyone was OK. He saw Michael, Stephanie, and Ronald, with coats on, just chatting together in the hallway.

When they saw Bill, they all just looked at him, smiled, and gave him big thumbs up sign.

Bill went to his office to get his briefcase and lock up. On his desk there was a sealed envelope, with *Bill* written on the outside.

Inside there was small piece of paper, with a short, handwritten note and a phone number. It read:

Dear Bill.

I want to thank you for our time together and for being so open to the new ideas. Good luck. I know that you're going to do great. Now go home and see your family.

Best Wishes.

Teacher

PS. If you ever care to meet me for coffee at Luna's, here's my number. Just ask for RD.

Epilogue

"You were right, Brian. That was some story. I can see how it changed your life. And I can tell you right now, it is going to change mine."

"So glad it hit you the same way, Walter. After I understood the lessons, I changed how I approached work and I started paying closer attention to everything around me and started seeing things I could improve for others."

"I then committed to those improvements and followed through. The results have been all good."

"That's so great, Brian. The first thing I'm going to do when I start my new job is to do nothing."

"What do you mean, Walter?"

"Normally, I would go in and put my head down and dig in. After hearing this tale, I'm going in to *stop*, *listen*, and *learn* and see how I might help others, and get them to help others as well. I want to create a positive and energized team, just like in the tale you shared with me today."

"That sounds like a great way to start, Walter. Please keep me posted as you go, and let me know if there's anything I might do to help. I'll be here for you, pal."

"I don't know how I can ever thank you, Brian."

"Well there is one thing you can do?"

"Name it, Brian."

"*Pass it on.*"

Acknowledgements

Many people are responsible for the final content of this book. First, we want to thank all the senior executives and managers who participate in our bi-monthly surveys, for they provide the knowledge of the underlying issues in the world of work today.

We also want to thank all those who provided encouragement in the early stages of this work, especially Wes Neff, Mary Frakes, Bob Yurkovic, Kim Barnes, and Art Cohen.

And thank you to all those business leaders who agreed to read the original manuscript and provide constructive feedback. All of your great suggestions were incorporated into the final copy.

So thank you to Alisa Oswalt, Tara Agen, Terry Ransford, John Jarvis, Don West, Doug Dreyer, Rod Sargent, Gerald Thompson, Michael Boylan, Karl Wolcott, John Orgizovich, Randy Lennon, David Symons, Shannon Ingram, Bill McBride, Carolyn Dickson, Peter McGinn, James Moore, Gregory Jones, David Bryant, Tom Murach, Timothy Smith, Micah Zeltwanger, Ken Myers, Bill Chamberland, Barbara Weaver Smith, David Aschenbach, Robert Wyatt, John Sircy, Tony Praza, Karen Liodice, Carol Rohm, and Edward Pease.

Also, thanks to Alvart Badalian at Arrow Graphics for designing all of what you see here and to Phil Martineau of NFI Research for conducting research and proofreading.

Most importantly, I want to thank my family, Teri, Ryan, and Chase, for allowing me the time and space to write this book. We did, in fact, take time to *stop* along the way, such as when Chase wanted to show me a new drum riff he learned, Ryan wanted to water-ski, or when Teri wanted to share her latest great painting. Thank you all.

About the Author

Chuck Martin is a bestselling author, speaker, and business strategist. Martin uses his broad experience and unique research platform to help companies understand and influence the factors impacting their business.

As the CEO of NFI Research, Martin is at the nexus of a global idea exchange and the leader of a research engine that regularly samples the mood and intentions of more than 2,000 senior executives and managers from 1,400 companies in more than 50 countries. The broad base of his network, the robust and virtually instantaneous nature of his process, and his experience analyzing results give him unusual currency and relevance.

A former vice president of IBM, Martin was the founding publisher and Chief Operating Officer of *Interactive Age*. He has been a journalist at five daily newspapers and has been editor-in-chief of four national magazines. He frequently appears on TV and radio, sharing his business insights.

Martin is the bestselling author of several books, his most recent being *Tough Management: The 7 Winning Ways to Make Tough Decisions Easier, Deliver the Numbers, and Grow the Business in Good Times and Bad*. Martin's audiences often rate him as the one of the best keynote speakers they've ever experienced. Attendees walk away with tools in their hands, ideas in their heads, and enthusiasm for what he's inspired.

The author resides in New England with his wife Teri and sons Ryan and Chase.

Coffee at Luna's

Find It

Stop, look, and listen to understand
what is truly going on

Change It

Commit to improve the situation by taking
concrete steps to improve what you see and hear

Pass It On

Clearly communicate the knowledge to others
so they can commit to improvement